Amazing Animals

ALLIGATORS
and
CROCODILES

Sally Morgan

W
FRANKLIN WATTS
LONDON • SYDNEY

An Appleseed Editions book

First published in 2010 by Franklin Watts

Franklin Watts
338 Euston Road, London NW1 3BH

Franklin Watts Australia
Level 17/207 Kent St, Sydney, NSW 2000

© 2010 Appleseed Editions

Appleseed Editions Ltd
Well House, Friars Hill, Guestling, East Sussex TN35 4ET

Created by Q2AMedia
Editor: Katie Dicker
Art Director: Harleen Mehta
Designer: Dibakar Acharjee
Picture Researcher: Maria Janet

ISBN 978 1 4451 0000 5

Dewey classification: 597.9'82

All words in **bold** can be found in the Glossary on pages 30–31.

Website information is correct at the time of going to press. However, the publishers cannot
accept liability for any information or links found on third-party websites.

A CIP catalogue for this book is available from the British Library.

Picture credits
t=top b=bottom c=centre l=left r=right
Cover images: Elizabeth DeLaney/Photolibrary, Shutterstock

James Robinson/Photolibrary: Title page, Yuriy Kulyk/Shutterstock: Contents page, Wando Studios/Istockphoto: 4,
Robert Nichol/Ecoscene: 5t, Cc. Lockwood/Photolibrary: 5b, Hansjoerg Richter/Istockphoto: 6t, Shelly Perry/Istockphoto: 6b,
Barry Hughes/Ecoscene: 7, Fritz Polking/Ecoscene: 9, Stan Osolinski/Photolibrary: 10, Brian Kenney/Photolibrary: 11,
Franco Banfi/NHPA: 12, Henry Ausloos/Photolibrary: 13, Fritz Polking/Ecoscene: 14, Philippe Henry/Photolibrary: 15t,
Fritz Polking/Ecoscene: 15b, Werner Bollmann/Photolibrary: 16, Jonathan & Angela Scott/NHPA: 17t, Fritz Poelking/
Photolibrary: 17b, Mark Deeble & Victoria Stone/Photolibrary: 18, Patricio Robles Gil/Photolibrary: 19t, Wh Chow/
Dreamstime: 19b, James Robinson/Photolibrary: 20, David M Dennis/Photolibrary: 21t, Dani/Jeske/Photolibrary: 21b,
Dr Myrna Watanabe/Photolibrary: 22, Dreamstime: 23, Mario Castillo/Reuters: 24, Roger De La Harpe/Abpl/Photolibrary: 25t,
Dr Myrna Watanabe/Photolibrary: 25b, Tobias Bernhard/ Photolibrary: 26, JTB Photo/Photolibrary: 27,
Wayne Lawler/Ecoscene: 28, Susan Flashman/123RF: 29, Shelly Perry/Istockphoto: 31.

Q2AMedia Art Bank: 8.

Printed in China

Franklin Watts is a division of Hachette Children's Books,
an Hachette Livre UK company.
www.hachettelivre.co.uk

Contents

Living dinosaurs 4

Body armour. 6

Swampy homes. 8

King of the Everglades: case study. 10

On the move 12

Surprise attack! 14

Time to feast .16

The Nile crocodile: case study 18

Sounds and signals 20

Life story 22

Under threat. .24

Saltwater giant: case study. 26

Facts and records 28

Glossary. 30

Index 32

Living dinosaurs

Alligators and crocodiles have been around for millions of years. They were living on Earth at the time of the dinosaurs. But when the dinosaurs died out, these **reptiles** survived! The alligators and crocodiles living today look very similar to their ancient ancestors.

Scaly-skinned reptiles

Alligators and crocodiles are the largest of the reptiles. They have four legs and a long tail. Their body is covered with a tough, scaly skin. They lay eggs like birds, but their eggs have a soft, leathery shell. Alligators and crocodiles are called **crocodilians**. There are 23 **species** of crocodilian including similar-looking reptiles called caimans and gharials.

 Most alligators are found in the southeastern USA. They tend to have a shorter, broader snout than crocodiles.

Tail is half the alligator's length

Largest scales are found along the back

Large mouth with about 80 sharp teeth

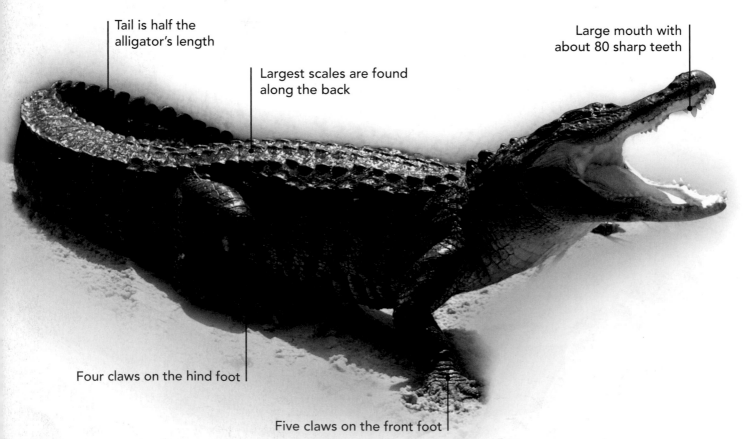

Four claws on the hind foot

Five claws on the front foot

Alligator or crocodile?

It can be difficult to tell the difference between alligators and crocodiles. One way is to look at the jaw. The crocodile's fourth tooth on the lower jaw sticks out (above). The snout is more pointed, too.

Large and small

The longest ever crocodile lived at the time of the dinosaurs. It was 12 metres long – about the length of a medium-sized swimming pool! Today, the largest is the saltwater crocodile that grows up to 7 metres, while the smallest is the dwarf crocodile at just 1.9 metres.

DINOSAUR TERROR

About 135 million years ago, animals living in the sea were terrorised by a vicious crocodile. It had the body of a crocodile but a head more like *Tyrannosaurus rex*. Its name was *Dakosaurus andiniensis*.

Dwarf crocodiles are the only crocodiles that leave the water at night to hunt on land.

Body armour

Alligators and crocodiles are fully protected by an **armour** of tough skin and bones that covers their body from nose to tail. This armour is thick enough to stop sharp arrows and spears.

Scales and scutes

The thick skin is made from a substance called keratin. This is the stuff that makes your hair and nails strong. It covers pieces of flat bone called scutes. The bones down the back are particularly large and thick for protection. A crocodile's back is tough and bony but the underside of the body is covered in small, smooth **scales** that don't catch on rocks or undergrowth.

Scales and scutes also reduce the amount of water lost from the skin

These thick scales provide a tough, protective armour.

The smooth belly scales slip easily over the ground.

Razor-sharp teeth are good for catching prey and tearing meat.

Growing teeth

A crocodilian's teeth are a bit like scales. They form from the skin as hollow, cone-shaped teeth without any roots. The mouth is armed with about 80 teeth and as one falls out, another grows in its place. Over their lifetime, an alligator or crocodile may grow up to 3,000 teeth!

AGEING SKIN

It is possible to age an alligator or crocodile by examining its scales. Every year, a growth ring (mark) appears on the scales. You can age the animal by counting the number of rings.

7

Swampy homes

Alligators and crocodiles love **swampy** places where there is mud and water. They like it warm too, so they are found mostly in **tropical** and **subtropical** regions, such as Central America and Northern Australia.

This map shows where crocodilians are found around the world. Crocodilians are crocodiles, alligators, caimans and gharials.

Crocodile homes

Crocodiles are found in the southeastern USA, through Central and South America, in Africa, and from India to Australia. One reason for this wide **distribution** is their ability to swim and survive in salt water. Crocodiles have a special salt **gland** on their tongue that gets rid of excess salt. The salt gland allows crocodiles to live along tropical coasts where there are mangrove swamps, on tropical islands, along rivers, and even in jungles.

Like other reptiles, a crocodilian's body temperature is similar to its surroundings. Warm, swampy conditions help them to keep active.

Alligator homes

Alligators are found in far fewer places than crocodiles. The American alligator is found only in the USA, while the Chinese alligator is found in parts of China. Their close relatives, the caimans, are found mostly in Central and South America.

LIVING TOGETHER

Florida, USA, is home to both the alligator and the American crocodile – the only place where these two animals are found together. This is due to the great variety of **habitats** – both salty and fresh water – and the tropical temperatures. American crocodiles can cope with more salt so they are found in mangrove swamps and saltwater creeks, while the alligators prefer freshwater pools and creeks.

King of the Everglades

When the Spanish first arrived in Florida, USA, during the 16th century, they found alligators living in the swamps. They called them '*el lagarto*', which means lizard, and over time this name changed to 'alligator'.

Clever camouflage

American alligators are only found in the southeastern USA, from North Carolina to Texas. These large reptiles grow up to 4.5 metres long and their colour varies. If they live in waters with lots of **algae**, they take on a green appearance, but those living in muddier waters under trees are darker. This helps to **camouflage** them in their surroundings.

 This alligator blends in with a log as it suns itself to keep warm.

Storing water

During the dry months, the water levels fall and some swamps dry up. The alligators make deep holes in the mud to collect water. These 'gator holes' are valuable sources of water for other animals, too.

10

A racoon is just a medium-sized meal for an alligator. Some attack prey as large as bears.

Large prey

Alligators are not fussy about their food. Some of the biggest alligators attack large **prey** such as black bears, pythons and even panthers. Most years, one or two people are killed by an alligator, usually when swimming. But alligators rarely attack people, unless they are disturbed or their young are threatened.

Success story

The American alligator was once hunted for its skin, which was used to make leather bags and shoes. These creatures almost disappeared but fortunately the US government acted to protect them. Since the 1970s, the number of alligators has increased and now there are more than one million in the wild, and many more in alligator farms.

On the move

Alligators and crocodiles look like lazy creatures that enjoy floating in water or lying in the Sun. But beware – they move surprisingly quickly when they have to!

Surging through water

Crocodilians are powerful swimmers. Their long tail propels them through the water at speeds of up to 20 kph. When they swim quickly, they hold their legs tightly against their body, to create a smooth shape that slips easily through the water. They stick out their legs to turn or brake. To dive, crocodiles and alligators breathe out to empty their lungs, and sink down. They use their legs to walk over rocks at the bottom of a river or pool.

Tail pushes body through the water

At slow speeds, only the tail moves from side to side. At higher speeds, the whole body moves with the legs tucked in.

Legs are tucked in so water flows easily over the body

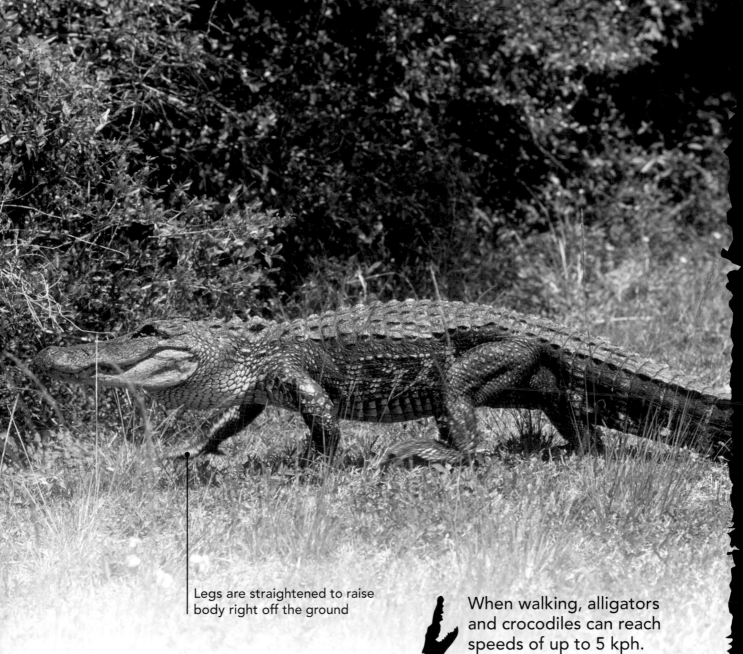

Legs are straightened to raise body right off the ground

When walking, alligators and crocodiles can reach speeds of up to 5 kph.

The high walk

Alligators and crocodiles can move quickly on land, too. Mostly, they belly crawl, using their legs to push their bulky body along. Sometimes, they do a 'high walk'. They straighten their legs and lift their body weight off the ground. This allows them to cross rough ground and clamber over wood and rocks. Some crocodilians gallop over the ground at speeds of up to 17 kph before they collapse. This looks a bit like a hopping rabbit, with both hind legs coming forwards together.

EXHAUSTED ALLIGATORS

Alligators soon tire after activity, so they lie around for hours, moving in and out of the shade to keep their body temperature at the right level.

Surprise attack!

Alligators and crocodiles take their prey by surprise. They lie underwater with just their ears, eyes and the tip of their snout above the water while they wait for unsuspecting prey to come within reach.

Powerful bite

These crafty creatures attack without warning, launching themselves from the water with a thrash of their tail. As they open their mouth, they grip their victim between their many teeth. The muscles that clamp the jaws together are so powerful, that the teeth can crush a turtle shell.

 An alligator lies in wait for prey to pass by.

When researchers move an alligator or crocodile, the jaws are tied for safety.

Death by drowning

With a firm grip on their prey, the alligator or crocodile dives under the water where it stays until the animal **drowns**. Alligators and crocodiles can swim under water with their mouth open because a flap of skin at the back of their mouth closes the opening to their throat. But they have to come to the surface to swallow. They either stick their head above water or drag their prey onto land for their feast.

This gazelle has been caught by the jaws of a hungry crocodile.

SNAPPING JAWS

Powerful muscles shut the jaws of an alligator or crocodile, but the muscles that open them are surprisingly weak. In fact, you could keep an alligator's jaws closed with just an elastic band!

Time to feast

As **predators**, crocodiles and alligators feed on many different types of animal. Small crocodiles feed on frogs, fish, snails and insects, while larger ones catch turtles, fish, small **mammals** and birds.

Smaller portions

A crocodilian's teeth grip and crush their prey, but do not slice it up. Instead, alligators and crocodiles swallow small animals whole. If the animal is too large to swallow, they tear it into smaller pieces. They do this by shaking and twisting their head, so that bits come off. Sometimes, they do a 'death roll'. They push one end of the prey's body under a rock or log and, while hanging on to the other end, roll in the water to twist a tasty piece off.

 A 'death roll' helps to break up large prey, such as zebra.

Acid stomach

Alligators and crocodiles deliberately swallow stones that collect in their stomach. The stones help to grind up food so that it can be easily digested (broken down). Strong stomach acids also help to digest flesh and bone. The stomach of an alligator has been found to contain nails, glass and bottle caps, but these cannot be digested.

 A twisting crocodile can break the backbone of its prey.

A crocodile may eat up to half its weight in just one meal.

The Nile crocodile

The Nile crocodile feeds mostly on fish, but attacks anything that ventures near the water. Sometimes, a group of crocodiles work together to catch their prey.

African giants

Nile crocodiles are the largest crocodiles in Africa. They can grow to 5 metres in length and weigh up to 1,000 kg. They live along rivers and lakes, and in freshwater swamps. During the summer, they dig burrows in river banks to escape the heat of the Sun.

This crocodile has pounced on a tasty meal as wildebeest cross the Mara River in East Africa.

Guarding nests

Nile crocodiles live alone for much of the year but they gather together during the breeding season. Unlike other crocodiles, the female buries her eggs in sand and guards them for three months. When the young crocodiles hatch, she digs them out and carries them to water. The young crocodiles stay close to the female for up to two years until they are ready to fend for themselves.

 Nile crocodiles gather together on river banks during the breeding season.

Crocodile god

In ancient Egypt, crocodiles were found along the River Nile. Many people working on or near the river were attacked. The crocodile was feared but also worshipped because it was a strong, fearless animal. Some crocodiles were kept in temples. There are even records of the ancient Egyptians keeping crocodiles in water-filled ditches around important forts and settlements as protection against invaders.

 This carving of a crocodile god was found on the walls of an old temple in Egypt.

Sounds and signals

Early explorers in North America were terrified by roaring and bellowing sounds coming from the swamps. These were the sounds of alligators talking to each other.

Chirps, roars and bellows

Alligators and crocodiles communicate using their senses of sound, smell and touch, as well as other forms of behaviour. The babies chirp in the egg when they are about to hatch so their mother can find them. Youngsters that are lost or in danger produce a distress call that brings the adults running. Adult crocodiles often roar when they are approached by another adult. Alligators and crocodiles also warn they are about to attack by thrashing their tail from side to side.

 Male alligators make loud bellowing sounds during the breeding season to attract females.

Showing off

The largest male in a group is usually the 'top' male. He shows off by swimming at the surface so that all the others can see the length of his body. A smaller male swims deeper in the water so just his head shows. Sometimes, the top males slap their heads against the water to make a noise, or they breathe out underwater to produce a noisy stream of bubbles.

The sounds this baby alligator makes as it hatches will help its mother to find it.

POPPING SOUNDS

Male gharials have a 'pot' at the end of their long thin snout, which they use to make a popping sound to warn off rivals.

Life story

Spring is a noisy time in the Florida swamps – this is the breeding season of the alligator. The males bellow to warn away other males and to attract the females.

Warm nest

After mating, the female builds a huge mound of grass, twigs and soil in which she lays up to 50 eggs. The mound is like a mini-compost heap. As the vegetation rots, it releases heat that keeps the eggs warm. She guards her nest for about 60 days. The chirps from the eggs tell her to dig out her young and carry them to water.

 An alligator searches her nest for her hatching babies.

When baby alligators hatch they are as small as a human hand.

Staying together

The youngsters stay together in a group with the female for about a year. They feed on small animals such as insects, shrimps, frogs and small fish. Unfortunately, these tiny alligators are preyed upon by other animals. Nine out of ten alligators will die in their first year. As they get older, they get larger and are safer from attacks. An alligator lives for about 30 to 35 years in the wild. They are ready to breed when they are about ten years old.

BOY OR GIRL?

The sex of a baby alligator depends on the temperature of the nest. More girls are born when the temperature in the nest is under 30°C and more boys hatch when the temperature exceeds 34°C. Both sexes are born in the middling temperatures.

Under threat

Around the world, many types of alligator and crocodile are becoming rarer and some are even at risk of becoming **extinct**. We need to act now to prevent these important species from dying out.

Hunted animal

Large crocodilians are dangerous animals and have been killed by people who fear them. But most are hunted for the smooth skin on their belly. Crocodilians are often killed at night because they are easy to find in the dark – their eyes shine in the beam of a searchlight like two red dots. This makes it easy to spear them between the eyes.

Tourist trail

The American alligator and the saltwater crocodile have been saved by hunting bans. Their numbers have increased and now many tourists travel to see them. However, other species are still at risk and more **conservation** is needed.

 Crocodile skin has been used to make leather bags and shoes.

Tourists bring money into an area which pays for the upkeep of nature reserves.

THE CHINESE ALLIGATOR

There are fewer than 200 Chinese alligators left in the wild. Their homes, in swamps and ponds beside the Yangtze River in China, have been turned into farmland. Fortunately, more than 10,000 Chinese alligators live in zoos and alligator farms, and these creatures could be reintroduced to the wild in the future.

Saltwater giant

The world's largest crocodile is the saltwater crocodile or 'salty' as it is called in Australia. Once there were millions of saltwater crocodiles, from India to Australia, but hunting has put this species at risk.

Valuable skin

The salty tops the charts for the number of people it attacks each year, so it is not surprising that people kill them because they are afraid. But saltwater crocodiles are mostly hunted for their particularly soft skin – the most valuable skin of all the crocodilians. Uncontrolled hunting between 1945 and the 1970s led to millions being killed. Today, some illegal hunting still continues in Southeast Asia.

 Some saltwater crocodiles are still hunted for their valuable skin.

International control

When their numbers began to fall, countries such as Australia introduced a hunting ban and there were international controls on the sale of crocodile skin. Since the 1970s, numbers in Australia have risen to about 300,000 saltwater crocodiles. However, saltwater crocodiles are still at risk elsewhere, especially in India, Thailand and Indonesia where few survive. This is due to the loss of crocodile habitat and illegal hunting.

Farm protection

In some places, saltwater crocodiles are raised in special farms for their skin. Surprisingly, this helps to protect the wild crocodiles, too. Crocodile eggs are collected from nests in the wild and the hatchlings are sold to crocodile farms. The money from the sales goes towards crocodile conservation. In India and Papua New Guinea, crocodiles have now been reintroduced to the wild with some success.

 This crocodile is being raised in a crocodile farm in Malaysia, and may return to the wild.

Facts and records

The largest of all the reptiles, alligators and crocodiles are feared around the world. They use their size and strength to kill their prey, but they are caring parents, too.

Largest and smallest

- The largest crocodile is the saltwater crocodile, which grows to 7 metres.

- The smallest is the dwarf crocodile at 1.9 metres.

- The largest alligator is the American alligator which grows to just over 5 metres.

- The largest ever crocodile lived about 110 million years ago. It was 12 metres long and eight times heavier than the saltwater crocodiles living today.

Crocodile tears

Legend has it that crocodiles cry when they eat humans. When a crocodile eats, its eyes froth slightly. Crocodiles huff and puff when they eat, and scientists think this pushes air into their tear ducts, producing more tears. This may explain the story of the crying crocodile.

The saltwater crocodile is the largest of all.

Body facts

- When an alligator or crocodile lies completely under the water, its ears are covered by tiny flaps and its nostrils close to keep out water.

- Alligators and crocodiles have a third, transparent eyelid. This protects the eye when the reptile is under water.

- At the back of the eye of an alligator or crocodile is a special reflective layer, called the tapetum, which gives them excellent night vision. It is this layer that makes their eyes appear red when they are caught in the beam of a torch or searchlight.

Names and numbers

- The Mugger crocodile gets its name from the Hindi word 'magar' which means 'water monster'. Muggers live in swamps in South Asia.

- Alligators and crocodiles live for up to 60 years, but some have been known to live as long as 130 years.

- During the 1950s, as many as 10 million Nile crocodiles were killed each year for their skin.

Did you know?

- Crocodiles sweat through their mouth. If you spot a crocodile lying with its mouth wide open, it is not being aggressive, it's just cooling off!

- A Nile crocodile called Gustave was believed to have killed up to 300 people during the 1990s. This man-eating crocodile was never caught, but its story was the basis for the film *Primeval*.

This crocodile looks threatening but it is just keeping cool!

Glossary

algae
simple plants, often single-celled, that live in water or damp places

armour
protective covering over the body, such as the scutes of a crocodile

camouflage
the colours and patterns on an animal's skin, fur or feathers that help it blend with its surroundings, so that it is hard to see

conservation
the protection of natural habitats, plants and animals

crocodilian
name given to crocodiles and alligators and other reptiles such as caimans and gharials

distribution
the geographic area in which an animal is found around the world

drown
to die in water when water rushes into the lungs

extinct
no longer in existence, having died out

gland
an organ in the body that releases a particular substance, for example the salivary glands in the mouth release saliva

habitat
a particular place where plants and animals live, such as a swamp

mammal
an animal that feeds its young on milk, and has hair on its body

predator
an animal that hunts others for food

prey
an animal that is
eaten for food
by another

reptile
a group of
vertebrates
(animals with a
backbone) that
usually have a
scaly skin, four
legs, a tail, and
lay eggs

scales
overlapping plates
that protect the skin
of fish and reptiles

species
a particular type
of animal, such
as a crocodile

subtropical
an area or climate
that is warm, lying
to the north and
south of the
tropical areas

swamp
a low lying area
of wetland with
trees and pools
of water

tropical
an area or climate
that is warm and
often wet, close
to the Equator
(the imaginary
line around the
Earth's middle)

Index

Africa 8, 18, 19
alligators 4, 5, 6, 7, 8, 9,
    10, 11, 12, 13, 14, 15,
    16, 17, 20, 21, 22, 23,
    24, 25, 28, 29
American alligator 9, 10,
    11, 24, 28
Australia 8, 26, 27

babies 20, 21, 22, 23
bones 6, 17
breeding 19, 20, 22, 23

caiman 4, 8, 9,
camouflage 10
China 9, 25
Chinese alligator 9, 25
communication 20, 21
conservation 24, 25, 27

crocodiles 4, 5, 6, 7, 8,
    9, 12, 13, 14, 15, 16,
    17, 18, 19, 20, 21, 24,
    26, 27, 28, 29

dwarf crocodile 5, 28

eggs 4, 19, 20, 22, 27

gharial 4, 8, 21

habitat 8, 9, 25, 27
hunting 5, 11, 14, 15

India 8, 26, 27

jaws 5, 14, 15

legs 4, 12, 13

Nile crocodile 18, 19, 29
North America 4, 8, 9, 10,
    20

prey 7, 11, 14, 15, 16,
    17, 18, 23, 28

saltwater crocodile 5, 24,
    26, 27, 28
scales 4, 6, 7
skin 4, 6, 7, 11, 15, 24,
    26, 27, 29
species 4, 24, 26
swimming 8, 11, 12, 15,
    21

tail 4, 6, 12, 14, 20
teeth 4, 7, 14, 16
threats 11, 24, 25, 26, 27

Web finder

Florida Museum of Natural History – Crocodilians
www.flmnh.ufl.edu/natsci/herpetology/brittoncrocs/cnhc.html
Learn about the 23 species of crocodilians and listen to their calls.

National Geographic – Reptiles
http://animals.nationalgeographic.com/animals/reptiles
Find out about reptiles and what makes them different to other animals.

San Diego Zoo – Alligators and Crocodiles
www.sandiegozoo.org/animalbytes/t-crocodile.html
Facts on crocodiles, alligators and gharials.

National Zoological Park – Reptiles and Amphibians
http://nationalzoo.si.edu/Animals/ReptilesAmphibians/ForKids/default.cfm
Fun facts, animals to colour, jigsaw puzzles and the story behind some reptile names.

National Biological Information Infrastructure – Reptiles for Kids
www.nbii.gov/portal/community/Communities/Plants,_Animals_&_Other_Organisms/
Reptiles/Reptiles_for_Kids
Information on all sorts of reptiles, stories in the news, photographs and fun facts.